Standard Nigerian Recipes & Their Health Benefits

Kalu Igwe Kalu

Standard Nigerian Recipes

Copyright © 2016 Kalu Igwe Kalu

Tel: +2348023572650

Email:passionintensified@gmail.com

All rights reserved. No part of this book may be reproduced or transmitted in any form or by any means, electronic or mechanical, including photocopying, recording, or by any information storage and retrieval system, without permission in writing from the author.

Published By Global Reach Publishing LLC

ISBN: 978-53176-1-7

ISBN-13: 978-978-53176-1-9

Printed in the United States of America

The views expressed in this work are solely those of the author and do not necessarily reflect the views of the Publisher, and the Publisher hereby disclaims any responsibility for them.

To God Be the Glory

INTRODUCTION

The taste of every Nigerian recipe brings a delicious experience. Each recipe is an irresistible one and it defines the Nigerian people. Most of these Nigerian recipes are prepared in other countries where Nigerians reside, in order for them to feel the sweetness of home food once again.

Knowing how to prepare meals yourself will enable you get the required nutritional values that these recipes are known to offer to the body. They aren't just sweet and tasteful as they may sound, but they are highly nutritious and highly medicinal. Eating outside the confines of your home is not advisable but learning how to prepare these recipes will give you a sense of responsibility in your home and the society.

Most of the foods cooked in Nigeria include plantain, rice, yam, beans and garri (*made from cassava powder*). These are mostly eaten with different soup and stew recipes.

CHAPTER ONE

How to Prepare Edikang Ikong Vegetable Soup

Vegetable soup is one of Nigeria's simple and easy to prepare soup recipes. It is usually eaten with garri or fufu (*made from cassava powder*) or wheat powder. Edikang Ikong is a delicious rich vegetable soup, commonly served as a top delicacy during very important occasions.

INGREDIENTS

Meat (*beef or cow meat*), snails (*washed with lime*), stock fish, whole dry prawns, cray fish, onions, periwinkles, pumpkin leaves and fresh water leaf (*washed*), palm oil and salt.

METHOD

- Wash the meat thoroughly and put in a clean pot;
- Add some seasoning to it, with some sliced onions ad little salt;
- Place on heat and cook for 35 minutes;
- Remove the snails from the shells and wash them thoroughly with lime to remove its moist from it;
- Wash the stock fish and soak in water, add little salt to it and leave for 5 minutes (*this will kill insects and remove impurities from it*), then rinse with clean water;
- Also wash periwinkles and prawns thoroughly;
- Add periwinkles, stock fish, prawns and snails into the pot of meat and cook for 12 minutes;
- Add the pumpkin and water leaves and mix;
- After 7 minutes add cray fish and palm oil to the mixture and leave for 10 minutes.

- Remove from cooker and serve hot with pounded yam or fufu.

HEALTH BENEFITS OF EDIKANG IKONG SOUP

- It improves digestion
- Improves circulation and blood production
- Improves memory.

CHAPTER TWO
How to Prepare Melon (Egusi) Soup

Melon soup is a recipe thickened by grinded melon seeds, also known as egusi. Most families, mainly from the Igbo tribe use this soup for traditional occasions.

INGREDIENTS

Fresh meat (*chicken, cow meat, goat meat can be used*), smoked fish, palm oil, sliced onions, chopped pumpkin leaf, salt, beef seasoning powder and grinded melon seeds.

METHOD

- Wash the smoked fish and use a pot to heat the palm oil.
- Using a different pot, steam the meat with a little onion, salt and beef seasoning to make the meat tasty;
- Pour the grinded melon seed into the heated palm oil and stir continuously for 10 minutes;
- Pour the steamed meat and its water into the fried melon seed together with the smoked fish and stir it once;
- Add some beef seasoning powder to the soup as it bubbles and leave for 10 minutes;
- Add the chopped pumpkin leaf to the soup and leave for 2minutes. You're done with cooking!

Melon soup is served with garri (*fried cassava powder*), wheat or pounded yam!

HEALTH BENEFITS OF MELON SOUP
- It serves as a supplement for fats and oil
- It helps in replenishing worn-out tissues and aids muscle formation.

CHAPTER THREE
How to Prepare
Goat Meat Pepper Soup

Goat meat pepper soup is sweet, nourishing and irresistible. It can be used as an appetizer and it's also appreciated because of its medicinal effect on the digestive system. It is a well known recipe and widely used as a cultural herb in most countries in West Africa.

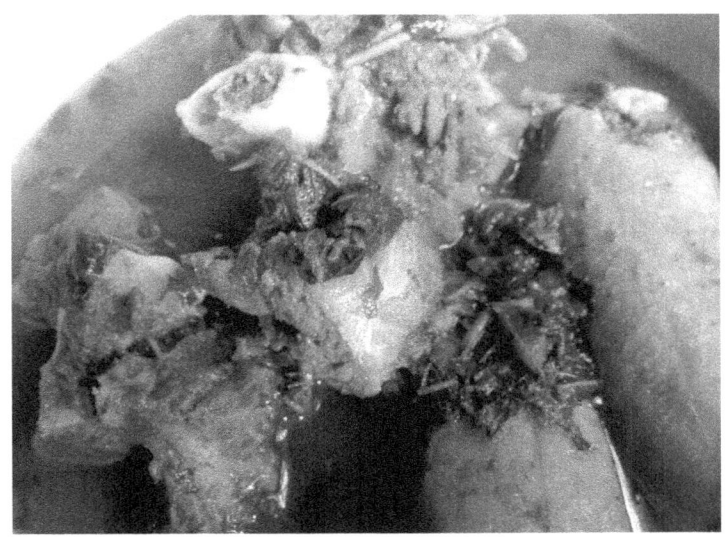

INGREDIENTS

Chili pepper, goat meat, dry uziza, 2bulbs onions, Grinded ginger, cray fish, salt to taste, beef seasoning and thyme.

METHOD

- Slice onions into tiny pieces;
- Rub the dry uziza continuously with your fingers to break into tiny pieces;
- Place the pieces of goat meat into the pot, put the pot on the heater and pour enough water to cover the content entirely;
- Add Chili pepper, dry uziza, sliced onions, grinded ginger, Cray fish, salt to taste, beef seasoning and thyme into the pot and allow cooking till it's done.

Goat meat pepper soup is mostly served with boiled yam.

HEALTH BENEFITS OF GOAT MEAT PEPPER SOUP

- Boosts appetite and reduces nausea;
- Flushes impurities in the blood stream;
- Helps for good digestion;
- Cures gastro-intestinal problems;

- Serves as an antibiotic against bacteria.

CHAPTER FOUR
How to Prepare Okro Soup

Okra soup is a fresh soup recipe prepared with okra and green vegetables. It is grown in West Africa. It can be grown in other regions around Africa and its environs.

INGREDIENTS

Okra, red palm oil, iced fish, salt to taste, grinded Cray fish, vegetable pumpkin leaves or spinach, beef seasoning.

METHOD

- Cut the okra into tiny pieces;
- Grind Cray fish to powder;
- Wash vegetables and cut into tiny pieces;
- Wash the ice fish properly, cut it and steam;
- Pour palm oil into a clean pot and heat;
- Add the okra into the pot and fry on low heat
- Add the steamed fish water into the pot little by little until you notice its becoming elastic (*the process shouldn't take more than 5minutes to avoid over-cooking the okra*);
- Add the cray fish, stock fish, pumpkin leaves, a pinch of salt and the fish and stir well (*cover the pot and leave to heat for 5minutes*);

Food is ready to be served.

HEALTH BENEFITS OF OKRA SOUP

- Source of vitamin and minerals.
- Clears the voice and the throat.

CHAPTER FIVE

How to Prepare Ewedu Soup

Ewedu soup is a type of soup prepared with the ewedu leaf and is mostly enjoyed by the Yoruba tribe in the western part of Nigeria.

INGREDIENTS

Ewedu leaves, local broom, locust beans, salt, water, potash, seasoning and stew.

METHOD

- Wash the ewedu leaves properly with plenty of water to remove sand;
- Place a pot on fire with water inside of it;

- Add the leaves into the pot and boil for 20 minutes;
- When it becomes soft, use broom to mash it very well;
- Add the salt and seasoning to it and stir;
- Leave to cook for 5minutes and it's ready to be served.
- Serve with wheat and stew.

HEALTH BENEFITS

- Source of vitamin and minerals;
- It helps in blood production.

CHAPTER SIX

How to Prepare Oha Soup

This is an Igbo traditional recipe. It is prepared with oha leaves and is very special because of the tender feeling of the leaves.

INGREDIENTS

Oha leaves, cocoyam, red palm oil, beef, stock fish, fresh pepper, salt, crayfish and seasoning.

METHOD

- Grind both crayfish and pepper and set aside;
- Wash, peel and pound the cocoyam to paste;
- Cut the Oha leaves with fingers into pieces;

- Steam the stock fish and beef with water and add some seasoning to it till it's done (*5minutes*);
- Add pepper and grinded cray fish and cook for 10minutes;
- Add the cocoyam paste into the pot and then together with the palm oil and salt to taste (*allow to cook for 15minutes*);
- Add Oha leaves and allow to cook for 5minutes;

Oha soup is usually served with prepared garri or wheat.

HEALTH BENEFITS

- Source of fats and oil;
- Repairs worn-out tissues;
- Acts as a supplement for vitamins.

CHAPTER SEVEN

How to Prepare Groundnut Soup

Groundnut soup is a tasty soup made from peanut paste.

INGREDIENTS

Chicken, onions, sliced fresh tomato, seasoning, 8 ounces of groundnut paste (*peanut butter*), salt and pepper and yam.

METHOD
- Cut onions and put in a saucepan of water and steam the chicken;

- Add groundnut paste and tomato and cook with low flame until the oil in the groundnut paste shows up;
- Fry the steamed chicken and add into the soup (*the chicken should be cut to hand full sizes*);
- Add the cut chicken to the mixture and stir. Leave for 20 minutes and then serve hot.

HEALTH BENEFITS
- High source of protein, fats and oil.

CHAPTER EIGHT
How to Prepare Nsala Soup

Nsala soup is a tasty, fast and easy soup recipe that has its origin in the riverine areas of Nigeria.

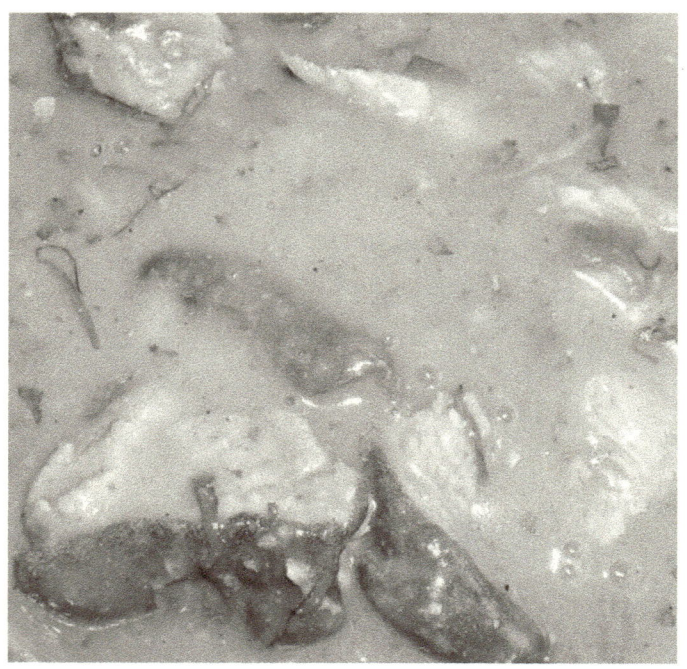

INGREDIENTS

Catfish, utazi leaves (*crongomena ratifolia*), raw sliced yam, chilli pepper, salt, grinded crayfish, seasoning. Utazi leaves is bitter in taste and is used only for flavoring, one or two leaves should be enough.

METHOD

- Cut the catfish into 1 inch thick size and wash carefully with hot water;
- Boil some cubes of raw white yam. When its soft, pound with a mortar till its smooth to paste then put it in a clean plate (*this is for making the soup thick*);
- Wash and cut the utazi leaves into pieces;
- Grind the pepper, crayfish and the utazi leaves and put each in a separate plate;
- Put the cat fish in a pot and steam with seasoning;
- When it's done, add crayfish, pepper, utazi leaves and the yam paste in small lumps;
- Add a little salt to taste and stir carefully.
- Leave to cook for 25 minutes and serve with pounded yam, garri or semolina.

HEALTH BENEFITS

- The presence of the utazi leave makes the soup a stomach cleanser.

CHAPTER NINE

How to Prepare Ogbono Soup

This soup is a Nigerian dish made with grinded ogbono seeds. It is used mostly in occasions to serve traditional guests and it is highly cherished by traditional elders.

INGREDIENTS

Red meat, grinded ogbono seeds, grinded crayfish, stocked fish, pepper, sliced onions, palm oil and salt.

METHOD

- Wash the meat very well and put in a pot;
- Add the sliced onions, pepper and water into the pot of meat and steam for 30minutes;

- Add the stocked fish and cook further for 10-15 minutes;
- Pour palm oil into a clean pot and fry the grinded ogbono seeds for only 3minutes;
- Gradually add the steamed water to it and stir until it draws and bubbles;
- Add the cooked meat, stock fish, pepper and crayfish to it and allow to cook for 10minutes.

When it is done, serve hot with pounded yam, garri or semolina.

HEALTH BENEFITS

- Helps to clear the voice (*mostly when mixed with okra*).

CHAPTER TEN
How to Prepare Banga Soup

Banga soup is a sweet recipe made from the sauce squeezed out from palm fruits and is full of great nutritional value.

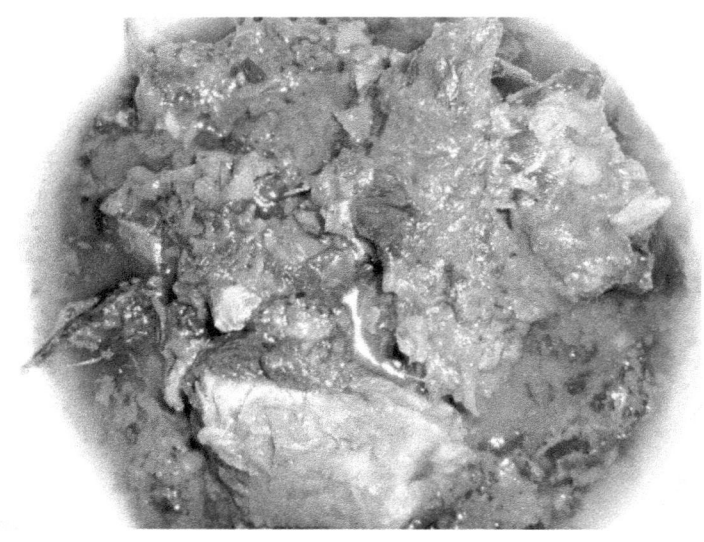

INGREDIENTS

Chicken or red meat, smoked and stock fish (*soaked*), bush meat, oil palm nuts, grinded crayfish, grinded melon, pepper, sliced onions, and salt to taste.

METHOD

- Steam the meat or chicken with salt, pepper and seasoning for 30 minutes;
- Add smoked fish and stockfish and cook for another 10minutes;
- Prepare the oil palm nuts to extract the oil from it (*this is done by boiling the washed nuts for 20minutes till it's soft*);
- Remove the water from the pot and pound the boiled nuts to remove oil;
- Use a sieve to separate the oil from the chaff;
- Pour the sieved palm nut oil into the pot of steamed meat together with the pepper, onions, and grinded melon;
- Add the crayfish and cook for 20minutes.

Serve banga soup recipe with semolina, garri or pounded yam.

HEALTH BENEFITS

- Banga soup is a source of fats and oil.
- It aids in the repair of worn out tissues.

Nigerian Rice Recipes

Rice is one of the most common recipes in Nigeria. It is a staple food eaten by most Nigerian families. It is the most preferred choice of food in major occasions in Nigeria.

Rice is cooked and eaten with any type of stew recipe or sauce when it is boiled without mixture and it can be cooked by boiling with other ingredients in one pot. Cooking rice mixed with other ingredients in the same pot is popularly called Jollof Rice in Nigerian terms. Rice is known to swell or increase in size just after boiling or parboiling.

CHAPTER ELEVEN
How to Prepare Jollof Rice

This rice recipe looks reddish in color. Jollof rice is cooked with other ingredients in the same pot.

INGREDIENTS

White rice (*4 cups of 400g or more*), freshly grinded tomato, vegetable oil, green beans, curry and thyme, 1 bulb of onion, garlic, beef spice, fresh cow liver, frozen or freshly killed chicken, salt, fresh or grinded pepper

PROCEDURE

- Parboil white rice for 30minutes and sieve out the water (*parboiling prevents the rice from sticking together when it's done*); we
- Steam the fresh liver and chicken with some sliced onions and garlic. Also add curry, thyme and little salt to taste (*steaming shouldn't take more than 25-30minutes*);
- Use a clean pot to heat the grinded tomato paste till its dry to paste;
- Fry the steamed chicken and liver lightly and keep in a clean bowl. Remember to keep the tasty water used in steaming them because it will be used in your cooking;
- Chop the liver into tiny pieces;
- Put another clean pot on the heater, pour some vegetable oil into it and allow to heat, pour the tomato paste into it and fry;
- When the oil turns very reddish, pour the water you used in steaming the chicken and liver into the mixture and allow to boil for 2minutes;

- Pour the parboiled rice into the pot and make sure the water covers the rice to the surface and leave till its dry;
- When its dry, add the green beans and fried liver to it and stir once;
- Food is ready.

Serve hot with fried chicken and a glass of fruit juice.

HEALTH BENEFITS

- Jollof rice makes you happy. It may be related to the release of oxytocin in the brain as our eyes register the pleasure that is a steaming heap of yummy orange rice. And fried plantain.
- It contains lots of vitamins and reduces inflammation, and heals infections.
- Rice is a well-known source of energy and fiber.
- It is a confidence booster.
- It prevents cancer.

CHAPTER TWELVE
How to Prepare Fried Rice

The Nigerian fried rice recipe is of high demand mostly in birthday parties, weddings and special events and occasions. It is not as reddish as jollof rice recipe, but it somehow has a yellowish-green color which makes it very attractive.

INGREDIENTS

3 cups of long grain white rice (400g), vegetable oil, frozen or freshly killed chicken, fresh cow liver, yellow curry and thyme powder, green beans (*a handful*), 4 medium carrots chopped to small sizes

(groundnut sizes), salt, sliced onions, beef seasoning powder

PROCEDURE

- Parboil the rice for 20-30 minutes and drain out the water with a sieve;
- Steam the chicken and liver with a clean pot using a pinch of salt, curry, thyme and beef seasoning powder for 30minutes;
- Sieve out the water used in steaming the chicken and liver and keep in a clean casserole dish to dry;
- Fry the chicken lightly;
- Chop the liver into smaller pieces;
- Take a clean pot, put some water into it, add some yellow curry powder to the water and set on the heater (*curry powder will give the rice a yellow-greenish color*);
- Pour the parboiled rice into the water and make sure the water is almost at the same level with the rice (*this should be done to make*

sure that all the water dries up by the time the rice is cooked and that the rice is not over cooked);

- Once the water dries up, transfer the rice to a clean wide bowl and ready to fry (the *whole rice won't be fried altogether, it should be done in sets, one after the other, so you need to divide it according to the size of the frying pan or pot you have. Also divide the condiments which includes green beans, sliced onions, chopped carrots and cow liver);*

- Pour some vegetable oil (*little*) into the pan and heat. When the oil is hot, add a part of the sliced onions and stir for 10 seconds. Also add a part of the cow liver, green beans and a part of the cooked rice;

- Repeat this procedure for the remaining sets and put each of the fried sets into a separate clean pot.

- Your fried rice is ready. Dish and serve hot with fried chicken at the side of the plate.

HEALTH BENEFITS

- Fried rice is source of fats, carbohydrates, protein, fiber.
- It contains lots of vitamins and minerals, and reduces inflammation, and heals infections.
- Rice is a well-known source of energy and fiber.
- It is a confidence booster.
- It prevents cancer.
- It helps the body by regulating blood pressure, stimulating the adrenal glands, relieving the body from cramps, diarrhea and dehydration and most importantly maintains fluid balance in the body.
- It plays a vital role in the excretion of wastes from the body and also plays a pivotal role in maintenance of blood pressure along with sodium.
- It produces collagen, protects the body from free radicals, ensures good cardiovascular and gum condition and supports the immune system.

CHAPTER THIRTEEN

How to Prepare Coconut Rice with Chicken

Coconut rice is a very tasty recipe with a captivating aroma. It is quick and easy to prepare. It is not a special traditional dish, but it is quite rich in taste and has more nutritional values.

INGREDIENTS

Long grain white rice, frozen or freshly killed chicken, grounded pepper, sliced onions, coconut milk, beef seasoning powder, salt, curry and thyme.

PROCEDURE

- Parboil the rice for about 30minutes with little salt;
- Steam chicken with beef seasoning, curry, thyme and little salt to taste. Steam for 30minutes;
- Fry the chicken after steaming and keep aside;
- Break two or more fresh coconuts, drink the liquid that comes out of it. Peel out the coconut from its shell and grind to pieces;
- Squeeze out the liquid (*coconut milk*) from the grinded pieces till the chaff is void of coconut milk;
- Pour the coconut milk into a clean pot, add some beef seasoning powder to it, some sliced onions, little salt and pepper;
- When the coconut water heats a little, pour the water you used in steaming the chicken into the mixture and allow to heat for 2minutes;

- After that, pour the parboiled rice into the mixture and make sure the water is a little more than the rice and leave till it's done;

Your coconut rice is ready to be served with fried chicken and cold fruit juice.

HEALTH BENEFITS

- Coconut rice is source of fats, carbohydrates, protein, fiber.
- It helps you loose weight.
- It contains lots of vitamins and minerals, and reduces inflammation, and heals infections.
- Rice is a well-known source of energy and fiber.
- It is a confidence booster.
- It prevents cancer.

CHAPTER FOURTEEN
How to Prepare Tomato Stew

Tomato stew is very simple and easy to make. This tomato stew recipe is not prepared with seasoning; it's just a base used for preparing other recipes such as making Jollof rice, coconut rice, spaghetti rice & beans, etc. Tomato usually has a natural sour taste, but this procedure will make it good for direct cooking.

INGREDIENTS

Tomato (*fresh and tinned*), vegetable oil and chopped onions.

PROCEDURE

- Wash and blend the fresh tomato. After blending, pour it into a clean pot and heat the tomato paste with high heat till all the water has dried;

- Open the tinned tomato and pour into a plate;

- Add the vegetable oil, chopped onions and the tinned tomato to the pot and stir very well. If the vegetable oil is excessive, pour out some of it and keep stirring the tomato while frying;

- When it looks a bit dry, take it out of the fire. If you're not using it immediately, allow it to cool. After cooling dish into containers and put in a freezer.

Like I noted above, you can use it to prepare any rice or spaghetti recipe.

HEALTH BENEFITS

- It helps you get healthy bones.

- It improves bone mass, fighting osteoporosis. It provides arterial protection. It strengthens the heart and protects it from diseases like blockage of arteries and stroke. It reduces the deposition of fats in the blood vessels, reducing bad cholesterol. It keeps your body fighting fit!

- It helps in the regulation of blood sugar.

- It can boost fertility in men. It helps to scavenge free radicals, which can cause infertility in men. So, if you are trying to conceive.

- It helps prevent the possibility of cancer in both men and women. It prevents breast, prostate, and colon cancer. It also protects the body from stomach and colorectal cancer.

- It promotes blood circulation, preventing anemia.

- It boosts to the nervous system.

- It activates the genes of the newborn cells, helping it grow to a mature tissue. It helps to keep the body healthy!

- It is rich in water and fiber that keeps you full for longer time.

CHAPTER FIFTEEN
How to Prepare Beef Stew

Nigerian Beef Stew recipe is made with tomato and other added ingredients. Apart from beef which is the main ingredients here, it can also be made with fresh fish.

INGREDIENTS

Tomato stew, beef, onions, chilli pepper, salt, fresh or tinned beef (*if the beef is fresh*), seasoning powder and thyme.

PROCEDURE

- Steam the beef (*fresh*) using 2 pinch of salt, thyme and pepper for 35minutes;

- Remove the steamed beef from the stock (*water used for steaming*) and pour the stock into a clean container;
- Since you already have your tomato stew ready, pour it into a clean pot and set on a heater;
- Add the beef stock to it (*make sure to remove any traces of little beef bones found in the stock*);
- Add some chilli pepper, steamed beef. Add salt if necessary and stir very well. Also add water and stir if the stew is too thick, cover the pot and cook with medium heat for 15-20minutes and it's ready.

Beef stew can be used to eat boiled white rice, fried plantain, and boiled yam.

HEALTH BENEFITS

- It helps you get healthy bones.
- It improves bone mass, fighting osteoporosis. It provides arterial protection. It strengthens the heart and protects it from diseases like blockage of arteries and stroke. It reduces the

deposition of fats in the blood vessels, reducing bad cholesterol. It keeps your body fighting fit!

- It helps in the regulation of blood sugar.
- It can boost fertility in men. It helps to scavenge free radicals, which can cause infertility in men. So, if you are trying to conceive.
- It helps prevent the possibility of cancer in both men and women. It prevents breast, prostate, and colon cancer. It also protects the body from stomach and colorectal cancer.
- It promotes blood circulation, preventing anemia.
- It boosts to the nervous system.
- It activates the genes of the newborn cells, helping it grow to a mature tissue. It helps to keep the body healthy!
- It is rich in water and fiber that keeps you full for longer time.

CHAPTER SIXTEEN
How to Prepare Nigerian Vegetable Sauce

The Nigerian vegetable sauce recipe is made from salad vegetables. It can be eaten with boiled white rice, boiled yam, fried plantain or even mashed potatoes. Vegetable sauce has a very attractive look and is rich in vitamins and nutrients.

INGREDIENTS

Chicken (*freshly killed or frozen*), vegetable oil, sliced spring onions, chopped fresh tomatoes, sliced carrots and cabbage, irish potatoes, chopped green pepper (*optional*), salt to taste and beef seasoning.

PROCEDURE

- Cut the chicken into hand full sizes and steam with some sliced spring onions, pepper, salt to taste and beef seasoning (*steam for 40 minutes*);
- Add the chopped fresh tomatoes and vegetable to the steamed chicken, cover the pot and cook for 15minutes;
- Add the carrots and cook for 5minutes;
- Add chopped tomato, pepper and cabbage, add salt to taste and stir the mixture and allow cooking for 5minutes. Ready to be served.

HEALTH BENEFITS

- Vegetable stew is a source of fats and oil.
- It aids in the repair of worn out tissues.
- It improves digestion

- Improves circulation and blood production.
- Improves memory.

CHAPTER SEVENTEEN
How to Prepare Mixed Vegetable Curry Sauce

INGREDIENTS

2 sliced carrots, 1 sliced onion bulb, 4 cut mushrooms, chopped green pepper, freshly killed or frozen chicken, corn flour (*thickener*), thyme, beef seasoning, salt to taste and curry powder.

PROCEDURE

- Cut chicken into handful sizes and steam with high heat. Add salt, little pepper, thyme,

onions and water to the chicken and steam for 30minutes;
- While steaming the chicken, mix the corn flour with water till it turns milky;
- After steaming the chicken and its well cooked, remove from the pot and keep the stock (*water used in steaming*) in a clean container;
- Add some curry powder, the carrots, pepper and mushrooms, stir and cook on high heat for 2 minutes;
- Add the mixed corn flour (*thickener*) and stir very well;
- Add the chicken to the mixture and stir. You can add more salt if necessary and that's all.

Serve vegetable curry sauce with boiled white rice.

HEALTH BENEFITS

- Vegetable stew is a source of fats and oil.
- It aids in the repair of worn out tissues.
- It improves digestion
- Improves circulation and blood production.

- Improves memory.

CHAPTER EIGHTEEN
How to Prepare Nigerian Egg Stew

Egg stew is very quick and easy to prepare. It is similar to tomato omelet, and they're both prepared with similar ingredients, but they are quite different. The difference here is this; tomato omelet has more of eggs while egg stew has more of tomatoes.

INGREDIENTS

2 Eggs, sliced fresh tomatoes, diced onions, salt to taste, chopped fresh pepper, vegetable oil and beef seasoning powder.

PROCEDURE

- Get a clean pot, pour some vegetable oil into it and heat;
- Add the diced onions and keep stirring for 2minutes;
- Add the tomatoes and stir for 5minutes;
- Add salt, pepper and beef seasoning to it and keep stirring;
- Break the eggs and pour into the mixture (*do not stir*) and cover the pot. Here, you'll notice that the eggs will form some lumps. When you see the lumps, stir a little and its ready.

Serve with boiled yam, boiled potatoes, boiled white rice or fried yam.

HEALTH BENEFITS

- It helps you get healthy bones.
- It improves bone mass, fighting osteoporosis. It provides arterial protection. It strengthens the heart and protects it from diseases like blockage of arteries and stroke. It reduces the deposition of fats in the blood vessels, reducing bad cholesterol. It keeps your body

fighting fit!

- It helps in the regulation of blood sugar.
- It can boost fertility in men. It helps to scavenge free radicals, which can cause infertility in men. So, if you are trying to conceive.
- It helps prevent the possibility of cancer in both men and women. It prevents breast, prostate, and colon cancer. It also protects the body from stomach and colorectal cancer.
- It promotes blood circulation, preventing anemia.
- It boosts to the nervous system.
- It activates the genes of the newborn cells, helping it grow to a mature tissue. It helps to keep the body healthy!
- It is rich in water and fiber that keeps you full for longer time.
- It is a source of vitamins and minerals.

CHAPTER NINETEEN
How to Prepare Nigerian Pepper Sauce

Nigerian pepper sauce has a sweet taste when eaten with boiled or roasted yam and boiled or roasted plantain. It is quick and easy to make.

INGREDIENTS

Fresh chilli pepper, onion, red palm oil and salt to taste.

PROCEDURE

- *Wash and chop the pepper and onions together and put in a clean bowl;*

- *Pour little salt and palm oil into the bowl and stir and it's ready.*

Unlike other stew recipes that go through heat, the Nigerian pepper sauce is fresh and doesn't go through heat.

HEALTH BENEFITS

- It aids in the repair of worn out tissues.
- It improves digestion
- Improves circulation and blood production.
- Improves memory.

CHAPTER TWENTY
How to Prepare Nigerian Beans

Black-Eyed or Brown beans are rich in high quality protein which provides a healthy alternative to meat and other animal protein. They are also rich in soluble fiber which helps lower blood cholesterol. This makes beans a must-have staple in Nigerian dishes. Still, beans Miss not a very popular food item because it is associated with flatulence and indigestion.

Allnigerianrecipes.com details some cooking methods that will help eliminate the discomfort associated with beans to ensure that this staple stays in your family menu. Studies have shown that beans can cause indigestion for most people. In this case, it is advisable to soak beans in eater for 5hours and properly washed. Then boil for 5minutes, throw away the water and continue your cooking.

HEALTH BENEFITS

- It helps you feel full.
- It helps the heart.
- It balances blood sugar.
- It cuts down cancer risk.

CHAPTER TWENTY-ONE
How to Prepare Nigerian Moi-Moi and Egg

Moi-moi is an irresistible Nigerian recipe prepared with beans. It is usually served with jollof or fried rice.

INGREDIENTS

Fresh black-eyed beans, beef spice, grinded Cray fish, fresh grinded yellow pepper, 2 sliced onion bulbs, salt and hard boiled eggs.

PROCEDURE

- Soak beans in cold water and leave for 8-10 hours to soften it;

- After this period, it must have softened. Without changing the water, wash the beans thoroughly with hands to remove the skin or layer. Then pour out the water and the removed bean layers. To remove more of the layers, pour enough water into the washed beans to cover the surface, you'll notice that the layers will come to the surface because they are lighter in weight.
- Sieve out the water and grind the beans with a rust-free grinding machine;
- After grinding, add some salt to taste, together with the sliced onions and grinded Cray fish. Also add the grinded yellow pepper and the beef spice to it.
- Add the boiled eggs to the mixture. You may prefer to slice the boiled eggs.
- After all ingredients, stir the mixture;
- Use an aluminum foil or plastic bowls and fill the mixture into each of them;

- Find a clean pot, pour some water into it. the size of pot to use depends on the quantity of moi-moi to be cooked;
- Use a metallic wire mesh base and spread it in the pot and heat. You can use a metallic wire mesh, pieces of aluminum foil or plastic bags for this;
- Begin to put each plate or foil of moi-moi into the pot. When you're done, cover tightly and allow to get done.

Serve hot using a flat plate and with any chilled fruit juice.

HEALTH BENEFITS

- It helps you feel full.
- It helps the heart.
- It balances blood sugar.
- It cuts down cancer risk.
- It promotes blood circulation, preventing anemia.
- It boosts to the nervous system.
- It activates the genes of the newborn cells,

helping it grow to a mature tissue. It helps to keep the body healthy!

- It is rich in water and fiber that keeps you full for longer time.
- It is a source of vitamins and minerals.

CHAPTER TWENTY-TWO
How to Prepare Beans and Plantain Porridge

Bean porridge is a very popular and quick to make Nigerian recipe. It usually prepared with plantain and sometimes with stock fish. It is advisable to use a black-eyed beans or a brown beans to make porridge because it will get cooked quickly.

INGREDIENTS

4cups of beans (*400g*), grinded crayfish, beef seasoning, fresh palm oil, 2 bulbs of diced onions, stock fish, grinded fresh pepper and sliced ripe plantain (*slice each piece to 3cm*).

PROCEDURE

- Remove all impurities from the beans and wash with hands;

- Wash stock fish and soak in warm water;

- Pour some water into a clean pot and place on your cooker;

- Pour the washed beans into the pot of water and allow to get parboiled for 30minutes;

- Once it's a bit soft, add little salt to taste and pour the fresh palm oil into the pot and boil for 20minutes;

- After this, pour the sliced ripe plantain and stock fish into the pot;

- Add the grinded crayfish, beef seasoning, grinded fresh pepper and diced onions, stir and leave for 15 minutes to get done!

Your beans and plantain porridge is ready!

Note: the plantain should not get too soft if it's over ripe and always serve hot!

HEALTH BENEFITS

- It helps you feel full.
- It helps the heart.
- It balances blood sugar.
- It cuts down cancer risk.
- Plantains are very reliable sources of starch and energy.
- It helps ensure healthy bowels and reduces constipation.
- It helps the body develop resistance against infectious agents and scavenge harmful oxygen-free radicals.
- It plays a vital role in the visual cycle, maintaining healthy mucus membranes, and enhancing skin complexion.
- It has a beneficial role in the treatment of neuritis, anemia, and to decrease homocystine (*one of the causative factors for coronary artery disease (CHD) and stroke episodes*) levels in the body.

- Plantains also contain folates, niacin, riboflavin and thiamin. Folates (*folic acid*) are essential for healthy pregnancy.
- It provides adequate levels of minerals such as iron, magnesium, and phosphorous. Magnesium is essential for bone strengthening and has a cardiac-protective role as well.
- Plantains have more potassium than bananas. Potassium is an important component of cell and body fluids that helps control heart rate and blood pressure, countering negative effects of sodium.
- Plantains are famed to be diuretic and can help prevent kidney and bladder problems.
- Plantains ease the discomfort associated with the menstrual period.

CHAPTER TWENTY-THREE
How to Prepare Beans Cake

Bean cake recipe is just like a snack. Usually eaten with bread. It is quick and easy to make at home. It is prepared by deep-frying with vegetable oil.

INGREDIENTS

Fresh black-eyed beans, beef spice, grinded Cray fish, fresh grinded yellow pepper, 2 sliced onion bulbs and vegetable oil for frying.

PROCEDURE

- Soak beans in cold water and leave for 8-10hours to soften it;

- After this period, it must have softened. Without changing the water, wash the beans thoroughly with hands to remove the skin or layer. Then pour out the water and the removed bean layers. To remove more of the layers, pour enough water into the washed beans to cover the surface, you'll notice that the layers will come to the surface because they are lighter in weight.
- Sieve out the water and grind the beans with a rust-free grinding machine (*it becomes pasty*);
- After grinding, add some salt to taste, together with the sliced onions and grinded Cray fish. Also add the grinded yellow pepper and the beef spice to it and stir thoroughly;
- Get a neat deep frying pan, pour enough vegetable oil into it and place on the heater;
- When it has heated for a while, put some whole sliced onion bulb into it (*this would give the oil a good taste for frying*);
- When fully heated and the onions in the oil is fried, use a wide-curved spoon, scoop out the

bean paste into balls one after another and deep-fry.

- When the balls are turned brown, then it should be removed from the oil with a sieve spoon and placed into a sieve pan for oil to drip down!

Your tasty bean cake is ready!

Always serve bean cake when it's hot.

HEALTH BENEFITS

- It helps you feel full.
- It helps the heart.
- It balances blood sugar.
- It cuts down cancer risk.

CHAPTER TWENTY-FOUR
How to Prepare Okpa

Okpa is known to have originated and eaten mostly by Indigenes of Enugu State, Nigeria. Preparing okpa recipe involves a few ingredients and it's quick and easy to make for public and personal consumptions. Most sellers of already prepared okpa recipe may not use the complete ingredients as it may be a little expensive to them.

It doesn't need much flavor although. If you reside outside Nigeria, you can place an order for okpa flour on Amazon. The flour is made from a seed known as bambara nuts, grinded with a machine. You can also ask family or friends to send you Okpa flour from Nigeria. You need to have the real taste of this delicious recipe by preparing it on your own at home. Let's try it.

INGREDIENTS

3 cups (400g) of okpa flour, banana/plantain leaves (*washed with salt water and heated with low flame for 20minutes. These leaves are used to wrap the okpa for boiling*), plastic bags can also be used as wrappers, red palm oil, beef seasoning, salt to taste, fresh grinded pepper and water.

PROCEDURE

- Sift the okpa flour into a big enough bowl to remove impurities;
- Add little salt and some beef seasoning to it and mix;

- Add the palm oil to the mixture and mix thoroughly till they are all blended together (*when it's well mixed, you'll have a bright yellow colored paste*).
- Pour some water into a clean big pot and set on a heater;
- When the water becomes warm, add some of it to the mixture and mix till there are no lumps;
- Add some salt to the mixture and scoop into the ready banana or plantain wrappers;
- By now the water in the pot should be in a boiling state. Add some spare banana/plantain leaves to the boiling water and make to settle at the base all over the pot (*this will prevent the okpa leaves or plastic bags where the okpa is contained to have a direct contact with the hot base of the pot*).
- Cover the surface of the pot with more leaves, close the pot tightly and cook with high heat for 40-45minutes or one hour at most.

- When the okpa is done, it becomes solid and ready to be served hot.

Note: after scopping the okpa into the banana/plantain or plastic wrappers, tie each base with a rope to prevent the mixture from gushing out.

HEALTH BENEFITS

- It reduces danger of stomach cancer.
- It has antimicrobial action.
- It is rich in lysine.
- It lowers cholesterol.
- It maintains healthy Bone.
- It is a source of protein.
- It fights kwashiorkor.

CHAPTER TWENTY-FIVE
How to Prepare Beans with Fried Plantain

Nigerian Fried Beans is so delicious that even those who do not like beans enjoy it! The closest Nigerian meal is Ewa Agoyin. All you have to do is make sure that every single bean seed is well coated with palm oil. So add enough Palm oil to the meal. Palm oil is good for you.

INGREDIENTS

Brown or black-eyed beans, 2 sliced onion bulbs, palm oil, beef seasoning, fresh grinded pepper, salt to taste, ripe plantain and water.

PROCEDURE

- Remove all impurities from the beans and wash with hands;
- Fry the plantain with vegetable oil and keep aside;
- Pour some water into a clean pot and place on your cooker;
- Pour the washed beans into the pot of water, add some salt and allow to boil till it's soft;
- Once it's soft, remove from the heater and put the beans into a clean container;
- Put an empty clean pot on the heater, pour palm oil and heat it up till the oil melts (*i.e. if it's congealed*);

- Add some sliced onions to the oil (*if it sizzles, then the heat is ready to be used*) and stir a bit;

- Add the fresh grinded pepper to it and stir for two minutes;

- Now, pour the beans and stir for three minutes (*add more salt if necessary*);

- Cover the pot and allow to simmer for about three minutes;

Your fried bean is ready. Serve with fried plantain by the side of the plate. Fried bean can also be eaten with bread.

HEALTH BENEFITS

- It helps you feel full.
- It helps the heart.
- It balances blood sugar.
- It cuts down cancer risk.
- Plantains are very reliable sources of starch and energy.

- It helps ensure healthy bowels and reduces constipation.
- It helps the body develop resistance against infectious agents and scavenge harmful oxygen-free radicals.
- It plays a vital role in the visual cycle, maintaining healthy mucus membranes, and enhancing skin complexion.
- It has a beneficial role in the treatment of neuritis, anemia, and to decrease homocystine (*one of the causative factors for coronary artery disease (CHD) and stroke episodes*) levels in the body.
- Plantains also contain folates, niacin, riboflavin and thiamin. Folates (*folic acid*) are essential for healthy pregnancy.
- It provides adequate levels of minerals such as iron, magnesium, and phosphorous. Magnesium is essential for bone strengthening and has a cardiac-protective role as well.
- Plantains have more potassium than bananas. Potassium is an important component of cell

and body fluids that helps control heart rate and blood pressure, countering negative effects of sodium.

- Plantains are famed to be diuretic and can help prevent kidney and bladder problems.
- Plantains ease the discomfort associated with the menstrual period.

CHAPTER TWENTY-SIX
How to Prepare Rice and Beans

This recipe is for those who cannot eat beans when it's cooked alone. This combination also reduces indigestion associated with beans when it's cooked with a staple food like rice.

INGREDIENTS

Rice, beans, tomato stew (*refer to tomato recipes*), fish or chicken, onion bulbs, beef seasoning

PROCEDURE

- Wash and soak the beans for 4 hours, throw away the water and boil till mildly soft;

- Wash the rice properly and parboil;

- After boiling both rice and beans, sieve out the water and set aside;

- Steam the chicken/fish using beef seasoning, salt, and thyme. If fish is preferred, steam for 5minutes;

- Pour the chicken/fish stock into a big pot (*depending on the quantity of rice and beans to be prepared*). Also note that it's going to rise during boiling;

- Add the tomato stew to the stock and stir for 2 minutes;

- Add the parboiled rice and cooked beans and make sure the water is not in excess (*this is to avoid over boiling*);

- Cover the pot and cook with medium heat till the water dries up and its ready.

It can also be served with fried plantain by the side of the plate and cold fruit juice.

HEALTH BENEFITS

- It helps you feel full.
- It helps the heart.
- It balances blood sugar.
- It is a source of energy.
- It maintains blood pressure.
- It prevents cancer.
- It is rich in vitamins.
- It takes care of your skin.
- It digests easily.
- It cuts down cancer risk.

CHAPTER TWENTY-SEVEN
How to Prepare Plantain

Plantains and bananas have similarities but unlike bananas, plantain can't be eaten in their raw state. Plantains are very rich in vitamins and minerals that the human body needs.

They are available at most grocery stores and can be eaten with lots of recipes. Most people eat plantain raw when it's ripe, while for others, it could trouble the stomach. Plantain can be fried, boiled or roasted.

PLANTAIN CHIPS

This can also be done for unripe plantain. Make sure the plantain does not get too ripe. Plantains that are just beginning to ripe are suitable for this recipe.

INGREDIENTS

Plantain (*ripe/unripe*), vegetable oil, salt to taste.

PROCEDURE

- Pour vegetable oil into a deep frying pan and put on a heater;
- Remove plantain from its back, slice thinly and put in a plate;
- Sprinkle salt to it and turn;
- Fry the plantain till it's hard and remove from the hot oil and keep in a metal sieve.

It can be eaten with any kind of juice or soft drink.

ROASTED PLANTAIN RECIPE

All you will need to do this is a barbecue set at a temperature of 120 C to roast the plantain.

INGREDIENTS
Ripe plantain (*unsliced*) and pepper sauce.

PROCEDURE
- Place ripe plantain (*as many as possible*) on the barbecue and roast;
- Keep turning the plantain to avoid it from getting burnt;
- You'll know it ready when it turns brownish in color.

Serve with pepper sauce (*refer to stew and sauce recipe*).

UNRIPE PLANTAIN RECIPE

UNRIPE PLANTAIN PORRIDGE

Unripe plantain is known to be rich in iron.

INGREDIENTS

Unripe plantain, red palm oil, onions, fresh pepper, salt to taste, pumpkin leaves and beef seasoning.

PROCEDURE

- Remove plantain from its back and slice into small chips;
- Wash pumpkin leaves, onions and fresh pepper and slice separately.

- Pour the sliced plantain into a clean pot, pour water and boil (*let the water be just 5cm high above the plantain surface*);
- When it's a bit done, add salt to taste and palm oil and leave to boil for 20 minutes;
- Add pepper, onions and pumpkin leaves, stir and leave to boil for 5minutes and its ready.

HEALTH BENEFITS

- It helps you feel full.
- It helps the heart.
- It balances blood sugar.
- It cuts down cancer risk.
- Plantains are very reliable sources of starch and energy.
- It helps ensure healthy bowels and reduces constipation.
- It helps the body develop resistance against infectious agents and scavenge harmful oxygen-free radicals.

- It plays a vital role in the visual cycle, maintaining healthy mucus membranes, and enhancing skin complexion.
- It has a beneficial role in the treatment of neuritis, anemia, and to decrease homocystine (*one of the causative factors for coronary artery disease (CHD) and stroke episodes*) levels in the body.
- Plantains also contain folates, niacin, riboflavin and thiamin. Folates (*folic acid*) are essential for healthy pregnancy.
- It provides adequate levels of minerals such as iron, magnesium, and phosphorous. Magnesium is essential for bone strengthening and has a cardiac-protective role as well.
- Plantains have more potassium than bananas. Potassium is an important component of cell and body fluids that helps control heart rate and blood pressure, countering negative effects of sodium.
- Plantains are famed to be diuretic and can help prevent kidney and bladder problems.

- Plantains ease the discomfort associated with the menstrual period.

CONCLUSION

Nigeria is rich and blessed with diverse kinds of foods with great people with wonderful cultural heritage. Each tribe, state or region in Nigeria is known for a particular type of recipe. People who live in the northern region of Nigeria (*mostly Muslims*) base their diets on beans, sorghum and brown rice, those in the eastern region base their diets on white rice, pumpkins, plantain and yams.

Anyone who feeds on these recipes for a period of 3 months will be free of detrimental health issues. Nigerian recipes are colorful, attractive and highly medicinal to human health.

It is very romantic when couples cook together. A couple that cooks together are happier and are more secured in their marriage. When couples cook together, it has a way of building trust in the relationship. This helps the couple to create a better knowledge of one another and also it elevates their marital relationship to a deeper level of intimacy.

We encourage couples to try out these recipes

together in the kitchen and they will see how romance will spring forth from this shared way of life.

www.ingramcontent.com/pod-product-compliance
Lightning Source LLC
Chambersburg PA
CBHW022122040426
42450CB00006B/811